D1274791

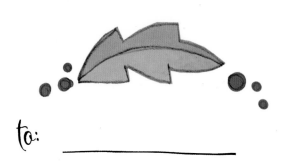

to: _____

from: _____

Published by Sellers Publishing, Inc.

Illustrations copyright © 2014 Robin Pickens

Sellers Publishing, Inc.
161 John Roberts Road, South Portland, Maine 04106
Visit our Web site: www.sellerspublishing.com
E-mail: rsp@rsvp.com

ISBN 13: 978-1-4162-4515-5

10 9 8 7 6 5 4 3 2 1

Printed and bound in China.

Seize the Moment:

Inspiring Words for the Journey Ahead

Art by ROBIN PICKENS

SELLERS
PUBLISHING

Potential

Each day
unfolds with
fresh new
potential.

Robin Pickens

It is better to be prepared
for an opportunity
and not have one
than to have an
opportunity and
not be prepared.

Whitney M. Young

Ready

Fortune

There never is but
one opportunity of a kind.

Henry David Thoreau

Genius is
99 percent
perspiration
and 1 percent
inspiration.

Thomas Edison

Inspiration

Perseverance

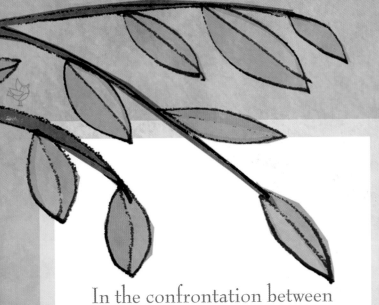

In the confrontation between
the stream and the rock, the stream
always wins — not through
strength but by perseverance.

H. Jackson Browne, Jr.

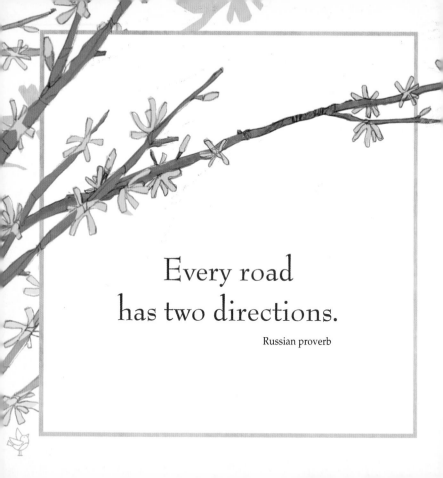

Every road
has two directions.

Russian proverb

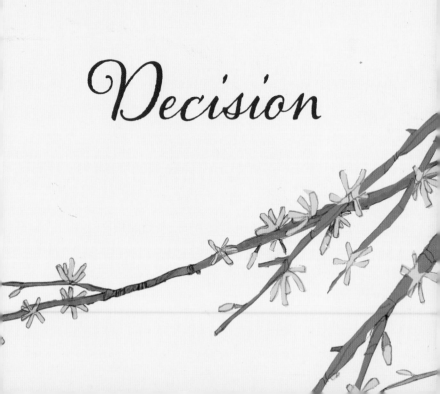

Decision

Possibility

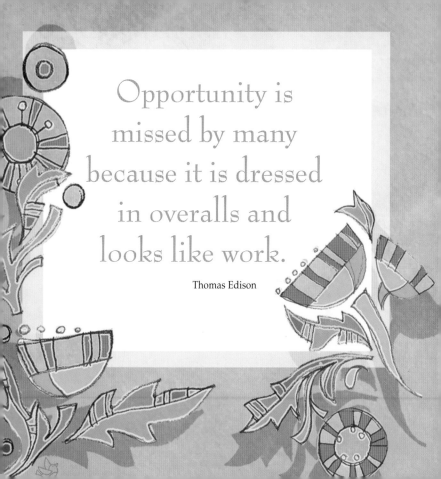

Opportunity is missed by many because it is dressed in overalls and looks like work.

Thomas Edison

When obstacles arise,
you change your direction
to reach your goal,
you do not change your
decision to get there.

Zig Ziglar

Hurdle

Hard work doesn't guarantee success, but improves its chances.

B. J. Gupta

Commitment

Purpose

You've got to get up every morning
with determination if you're going
to go to bed with satisfaction.

George Horace Lorimer

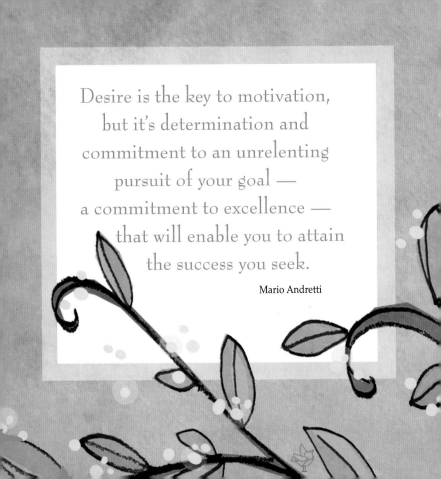

Desire is the key to motivation,
but it's determination and
commitment to an unrelenting
pursuit of your goal —
a commitment to excellence —
that will enable you to attain
the success you seek.

Mario Andretti

Resolve

Far and away the
best prize that life
offers is the chance
to work hard at
work worth doing.

Theodore Roosevelt

Every day is filled with
exploration and
the chance to
discover something
wonderful.

Robin Pickens

Explore

Insight

Little gifts of discovery await you today.

Robin Pickens

Discover a new part of you.
Try a different approach, a lighter attitude,
a fresh outlook. Every day is a chance
to reinvent yourself.

Robin Pickens

Delight

Courage

Don't let the fear of striking out hold you back.

Babe Ruth

Experience is
a hard teacher
because she gives
the test first,
the lesson
afterwards.

Vernon Sanders Law

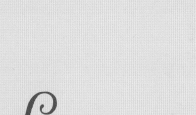

Lesson

Knowledge

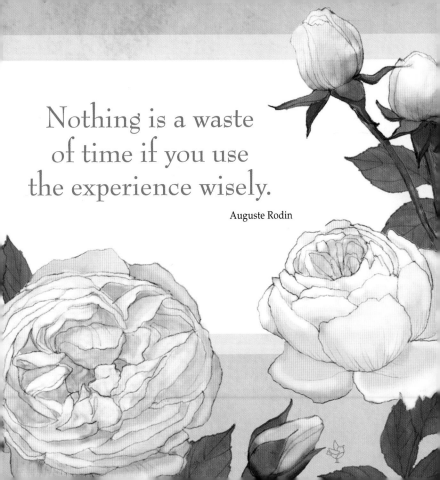

Nothing is a waste
of time if you use
the experience wisely.

Auguste Rodin

Do not let making
a living prevent you
from making a life.

John Wooden

Happiness

Success

Don't wait until everything is just right. It will never be perfect. There will always be challenges, obstacles, and less-than-perfect conditions. So what. Get started now. With each step you take, you will grow stronger and stronger, more and more skilled, more and more self-confident, and more and more successful.

Mark Victor Hansen

Defeat should never be a source of discouragement, but rather a fresh stimulus.

Bishop Robert South

Encouragement

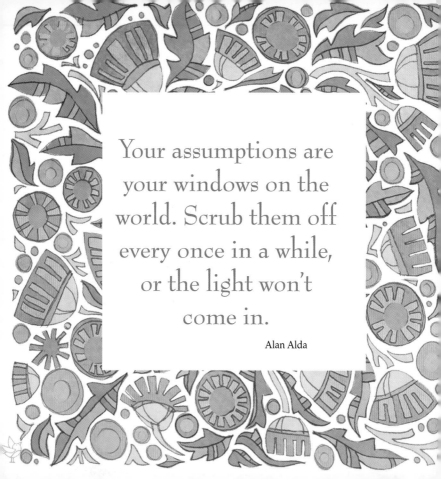

Your assumptions are your windows on the world. Scrub them off every once in a while, or the light won't come in.

Alan Alda

Awareness

Magic

Somewhere, something incredible is waiting to be known.

Dr. Carl Sagan

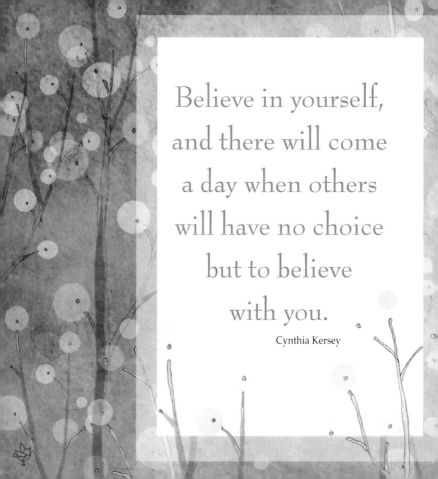

Believe in yourself,
and there will come
a day when others
will have no choice
but to believe
with you.

Cynthia Kersey

Confidence

Believe

The height of your accomplishments will equal the depth of your convictions.

William F. Scolavino

Someone with their feet planted firmly on the ground has no hope of reaching the stars.

Kelsey Dunn

Reach

Pursue

Follow your passion,
listen to your heart,
make every day a celebration
of your vision and soul.

Robin Pickens

Be bold!
Shine with
all your
color and
character.

Robin Pickens

Shine

Seek

We are each
    gifted in a unique
        and important way.
            It is our privilege and
                our adventure to
                    discover our own
                        special light.

Mary Dunbar

Fly high.
Be brilliant.
Celebrate all your
accomplishments.

Robin Pickens

Celebrate